Seeing the Future

The Final Vision of Sitting Bull

Jennifer Silate

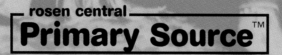

rosen central
Primary Source™

The Rosen Publishing Group, Inc., New York

Published in 2004 by The Rosen Publishing Group, Inc.
29 East 21st Street, New York, NY 10010

Editor: Scott Waldman
Book Design: Mork Liu
Photo Researcher: Rebecca Anguin-Cohen

Photo Credits: Cover (left) and p. 31 Joslyn Art Museum, Omaha, Nebraska; cover (right) illustration
© Debra Wainwright/The Rosen Publishing Group; title page (#A2952), pp. 6 (#C3632),
18, (#0036-082), 29 (#A2952) State Historical Society of North Dakota; pp. 10, 14, 30 Minnesota
Historical Society Collections; p. 22 Library of Congress Prints and Photographs Division;
p. 32 © Corbis

First Edition

Library of Congress Cataloging-in-Publication Data

Silate, Jennifer.
    Seeing the future : the final vision of Sitting Bull / Jennifer
    Silate.
    v. cm.—(Great moments in American history)
    Contents: Life at Standing Rock — The dance of the ghost —Watching
    the dance — A plan to arrest — Death from his people.
    ISBN 0-8239-4384-4 (lib. bdg.)
    1. Sitting Bull, 1834?-1890—Juvenile literature. 2. Ghost
    dance—Juvenile literature. 3. Dakota Indians—Biography—Juvenile
    literature. [1. Sitting Bull, 1834?-1890. 2. Dakota Indians—Biography.
    3. Indians of North America—Great Plains—Biography. 4. Kings, queens,
    rulers, etc. 5. Ghost dance.] I. Title. II. Series.

    E99.DIS47 2004
    978.004'9752'0092--dc21

                                                2003002687

Manufactured in the United States of America

CONTENTS

Preface

*I*n 1874, gold was found in the Black Hills of South Dakota. The Black Hills were a holy place for the Sioux Indians who lived there. The U.S. government wanted to buy the land from the Sioux, but they would not sell it. Earlier treaties between the government and Native Americans did not let any white settlers into that area. However, the government began to allow people to enter the Black Hills to search for gold. The government wanted the Native Americans to leave the area. Sitting Bull, the head chief of the Lakotas—a tribe of Sioux Indians—did not want to leave his homeland with his followers. Government soldiers tried to force Sitting Bull and his people to live on reservations. In May 1877, Sitting Bull and his followers fled to Canada.

For hundreds of years, the Sioux had hunted buffalo for food, clothes, and shelter. But by 1881, most of the buffalo in the United States and Canada were gone. They had been over-hunted for many years. As a result, Sitting Bull's people were starving. He and his people returned to the United States to live on a reservation. There, they would get enough food to live. First, he went to Fort Buford, Montana. Then he was held as a prisoner of war for two years at Fort Randall. Finally, he and his followers were forced to make the journey to a reservation called Standing Rock on the border of North and South Dakota.

Sitting Bull and his people would not be allowed to leave Standing Rock. As he made his way to the reservation, Sitting Bull sadly wondered if his people would be able to live under the white man's rules. If they couldn't, he feared terrible things would happen....

Sitting Bull (front left) meets with James McLaughlin (front right) at Standing Rock in 1886. Standing Rock was named for the rock formation in the center of the photo. If viewed from the side, the rock looks like a Native American woman with a child on her back.

LIFE AT STANDING ROCK

On May 10, 1883, Sitting Bull and 172 of his people shuffled off of the *Behan* steamboat in Standing Rock, North Dakota. Tall, white buildings with large, glass windows towered over the parade of Sioux men, women, and children as they walked the dusty road to the Standing Rock agency. The agency was where the people who supervised a reservation lived.

The Indian agent for Standing Rock was named James McLaughlin. McLaughlin greeted Sitting Bull and asked him to come inside. Before McLaughlin sat down, Sitting Bull said, "As Chief, I would like to pass out food and supplies to each family. I know that normally you have that duty. However, I know what is best for my people and what they need. Also, I know that we must learn to

7

farm. I think I will speak to the others living here who are already farming and see what they do. Perhaps next year I will plant a crop."

"SIR!" McLaughlin exploded, "You will be treated the same as everyone else here. Every other Saturday, you will receive only your share of food and supplies. If you want vegetables, grow them. There are rules here in Standing Rock and you must follow them!"

Sitting Bull was shocked. No one had ever spoken to him with such disrespect. He stormed out of McLaughlin's office. Even though it hurt him to do so, he had to obey McLaughlin's orders. If he didn't set a peaceful example for his people, a war could break out. Within a week, Sitting Bull started to farm.

For the next few years, things were quiet on the reservation. Sitting Bull built a cabin close to the Grand River, near where he was born. It was hard for him and his people to stay in one place since they were used to moving their homes often. They worked hard growing corn,

oats, and potatoes and raising chickens, cows, and horses. It seemed like they might actually be able to live on the reservation for a long time.

Then one morning Sitting Bull woke before the sun rose. He was upset, though he did not know why. He walked out onto the prairie. The sun was beginning to rise. The purple sky was streaked with orange and red. Sitting Bull walked up a small hill and looked at the sky. Suddenly, he heard a low voice. It was coming toward him. A few feet away, Sitting Bull saw a small, yellow bird. It seemed to be glowing. The bird was a meadowlark. The meadowlark spoke to Sitting Bull.

"Your people will kill you," it said to the great chief.

Sitting Bull believed what the meadowlark said. According to the Sioux, meadowlarks were very wise and spoke the Lakota language. Sitting Bull was puzzled. Why would his own people kill him?

The beef rations given to the Native Americans at Standing Rock did not provide them with as much food as buffalo hunts in their tribal lands.

Chapter Two

THE DANCE OF THE GHOST

*I*n the years that followed, Sitting Bull worked on his farm. Then, in 1889, the U.S. government sent a group of men to Standing Rock. They wanted the Native Americans to sign an agreement that would force them to sell 9 million acres of land. The men promised the Native Americans a fair price for their land. Sitting Bull was against the idea, but he could not stop others from signing. Two weeks after the agreement was signed, the people's supply of beef was cut by the government. The winter was very bad that year. Diseases swept through the reservations. Many people died. Sitting Bull's people were hungry and sick.

Those who survived the winter of 1889-90 worked through the spring, planting crops.

Yet the summer was just as hard as the winter. Summer heat destroyed the Native Americans' crops. Fall brought cooler winds as well as a Lakota Indian named Kicking Bear, from the Cheyenne River. Kicking Bear brought news that promised to change everyone's life.

The people in Sitting Bull's reservation gathered around the young man as he spoke.

"I have met a holy man named Wovoka," Kicking Bear started. "He had a vision that the day of the white man will end. A great being will come and cover the earth with fresh dirt. New trees and green grasses will grow. Fresh, clean water will flow. The buffalo will return and everyone who has died will return, to live again in paradise."

People looked around at each in disbelief. Could Kicking Bear's words be true?

"This spring, everyone who has done the Ghost Dance will be taken to this new world. Those who do not dance will be left here, in misery. Do the dance of the ghost all winter long."

Kicking Bear lifted up a shirt. The shirt was long, with flowing sleeves. There were moons, stars, and birds painted on it and fringe along the bottom.

"Wear the Ghost Shirt," Kicking Bear said. "You will be safe from the white man's bullets. Nothing will harm you."

The people in Sitting Bull's settlement were excited. If Kicking Bear told the truth, they would soon find an end to their sadness. They began dancing.

One Bull, Sitting Bull's nephew, wasn't so pleased though. He was an Indian police officer who worked for McLaughlin. One Bull ran to tell McLaughlin what Kicking Bear had said.

McLaughlin let out a tired sigh as he listened to One Bull. He knew that the Ghost Dance could mean trouble. Excited Lakotas doing the dance wouldn't want to obey his rules.

"Tell me everything," McLaughlin said as he picked up his gun and cleaned it.

The Ghost Dance was very important to Native Americans. Photographs of the ceremony were not allowed. To get this picture, a reporter snuck a camera in under his coat.

Chapter Three

WATCHING THE DANCE

On November 17, James McLaughlin went to Sitting Bull's settlement to see what the Ghost Dance was all about. McLaughlin saw a great crowd of people around a tall pole. The pole was decorated with colored cloths and feathers. About one hundred people were dancing. They were all wearing their Ghost Shirts. The dancers held hands, jumped, and spun in a circle around the pole. Another one hundred people watched the dancers.

Sitting Bull watched the dancers. He did not dance. Another Lakota, Bull Ghost, was in charge of the dance. The dancers chanted and yelled. McLaughlin went back home. He knew that the dancers were very excited. If he tried to talk to Sitting Bull now, he was sure to run into trouble.

McLaughlin returned to Sitting Bull's settlement the next morning. "Sitting Bull," McLaughlin started, "I want to talk to you about the Ghost Dance. You should not let your people do it. It is only going to hurt them."

"I do not believe you," replied Sitting Bull. "The Ghost Dance gives them hope. We have our religion. You have yours. The dancers are not hurting anyone. Let them be."

"The dancers here may be peaceful, but they have stopped working on their homes and farms," argued McLaughlin. "All they do is dance. You should stop this before it gets worse. Besides, you cannot believe that it will work."

"I do not know if it will work. But I will not take away my people's hopes and dreams," Sitting Bull said angrily.

"Why don't you come to the agency and we can talk about it? Give me one night. I will change your mind about the Ghost Dance," responded McLaughlin.

"Maybe I will come to the agency next Saturday," said Sitting Bull as he was getting out of the wagon. "Goodbye, Agent McLaughlin."

Sitting Bull never went to go see Agent McLaughlin. On November 20, government soldiers went to other reservations to stop the Ghost Dance. Sitting Bull sent Strikes-the-Kettle to pick up his beef supply on Saturday. He told McLaughlin that one of Sitting Bull's children was sick and the chief couldn't come. However, more than twenty other men from the Grand River area didn't come that Saturday, too. They sent their wives instead. Agent McLaughlin was angry. He refused to give the women the beef and ordered the men to come get it.

That night McLaughlin couldn't sleep because the situation on the reservation was getting tense. If all the Native Americans who lived there rose against him, McLaughlin knew that neither he nor his men would survive a fight.

Agent McLaughlin always treated Sitting Bull just as any other person on his reservation, rather than as a great leader.

Chapter Four

A PLAN TO ARREST

O n the evening of December 12, 1890, Bull Ghost, the Ghost Dance director, delivered a letter to Agent McLaughlin. The letter was from Sitting Bull. In the letter, Sitting Bull asked to go to the Pine Ridge reservation. Sitting Bull wanted to learn from Ghost Dance teachers at Pine Ridge.

McLaughlin crushed the note in his hand.

"Sitting Bull will not leave the reservation," he said.

"Sitting Bull told me that if you do not give him a pass, he will still go," explained Bull Ghost. "He believes that this dance is important for the survival of his people. He is too proud to let this dance be taken away from them like their land has been."

"Come back tomorrow. I'll have a letter for you

to take to Sitting Bull!" McLaughlin screamed as he pushed Bull Ghost out of the door.

After Bull Ghost left, McLaughlin sat at his desk and wrote to Sitting Bull:

Sitting Bull:

Do not go to Pine Ridge. Do not go to any other reservations. Send the dancers back to their homes. The rules on this reservation must be followed. It is my job to make sure that they are followed, one way or another.

James McLaughlin

At 4:00 P.M., two days later, Agent McLaughlin was alone in his office. He was trying to think up a plan to safely arrest Sitting Bull. In the past few weeks, the Ghost Dance had become more dangerous on the Pine Ridge and Rosebud reservations. After the soldiers had moved into reservations, the dancers fled. They danced on a cliff out of the soldiers' reach. The soldiers were trying to get the dancers down without having to fight. They were in a stand-off. Now, Sitting Bull wanted to go there, too.

McLaughlin felt that Sitting Bull should be removed at once from the reservation so that things would not get out of control with the Ghost Dance. He wanted to get him out peacefully. But how? A knock on the door interrupted McLaughlin's thoughts.

It was a messenger with news from Lieutenant Bull Head. He had sent spies into Sitting Bull's settlement. The spies reported that Sitting Bull planned to leave for Pine Ridge in a few mornings. Bull Head wanted permission to arrest Sitting Bull before he could get away. As McLaughlin read the letter, his commander, General Drum, entered. General Drum had received orders from an even higher military officer in Chicago, Illinois, to arrest Sitting Bull. McLaughlin and Drum agreed to arrest Sitting Bull the next morning. McLaughlin was hoping that the arrest would go smoothly, but he knew Sitting Bull was a proud and powerful man. He would not likely go down without a fight.

Sitting Bull may have traveled all around the United States during his lifetime, but he left the world at the same spot where he entered it. The cabin where Sitting Bull was arrested on the morning of his death was built on the spot where he was born fifty-nine years before.

Chapter Five

DEATH FROM HIS PEOPLE

McLaughlin and Drum ordered Bull Head to lead all of the Grand River Indian police into Sitting Bull's settlement the next morning. It was a smart plan. The Ghost Dancers might attack soldiers, but they probably would not attack their own people. McLaughlin and Drum also ordered two troops of cavalry to back up the police. Bull Head gathered the Indian police in his cabin. His cabin was built on the site where Sitting Bull had been born fifty-nine years before. Some of the police, including Bull Head himself, had lived and fought beside Sitting Bull. Many were sad about what they had to do the next morning.

The men finally set off at 4:30 A.M., December 15, 1890. It was cold and rainy. Forty-three Native American men were on their way to arrest

Sitting Bull. At 6:00 A.M., the band of men reached Sitting Bull's settlement. Barking dogs told of the men's arrival.

The men beat on the door of Sitting Bull's cabin, shouting his name. Sitting Bull was asleep. Before he could get up, three men stormed into his room. Lieutenant Bull Head, Sergeant Shave Head, and Red Tomahawk were all Lakota Indians.

"We have come for you, Sitting Bull," said Bull Head from the shadows. Lieutenant Bull Head and Sergeant Shave Head each grabbed Sitting Bull. Red Tomahawk pushed Sitting Bull from behind.

When the four men reached the doorway, they were met by an angry mob. Catch-the-Bear, one of Sitting Bull's long-time friends— and one of Bull Head's long-time enemies— pushed his way to the front of the crowd.

"What do you think you're doing?" Catch-the-Bear asked the men angrily. "They can't take him from us!" he yelled at the crowd.

People tried to press past the line of police that were guarding the cabin.

They yelled at the police.

"We won't let you take him!" they screamed.

In the confusion, the police struggled to keep the crowd in control. They put Sitting Bull on a waiting horse.

CRACK!

Catch-the-Bear fired his rifle at Bull Head, hitting him in his side. As Bull Head fell, he turned and fired his gun at Sitting Bull.

Sitting Bull was hit in the chest. Red Tomahawk fired another bullet into the back of Sitting Bull's head. Sitting Bull dropped to the ground. In a pool of his own blood, the great chief died.

Sitting Bull's followers angrily attacked the police. Bullets flew in every direction. The fighting only lasted for about half an hour. When it ended, Sitting Bull, his son Crow Foot, and Catch-the-Bear were all dead. Eight Native Americans and five members of the

police died that day. Later, another two police-
men would die from their wounds.

The cavalry troops that had been sent as
backup soon arrived on the scene. Bodies lay
everywhere. The sound of their families crying
in horror filled the air. No Ghost Dancers were
to be found though. They had quickly left their
homes and moved on.

On January 2, 1891 a group of Lakota
returned to Sitting Bull's settlement to bury the
dead. White willow stakes had been stuck into
the ground by the Ghost Dancers to mark the
place where the police and the dancers had fall-
en. The Native Americans buried all the bodies
they could find. Sitting Bull's body was not
there, though. Earlier, McLaughlin had Sitting
Bull's body placed in an unmarked grave.

The great leader of the Lakotas left his world
exactly as he knew he would—cut down by his
own people. Sitting Bull's vision had finally
come true.

GLOSSARY

agent (AY-juhnt) someone who works for the government

arrest (uh-REST) to stop and hold someone by the power of law

government (GUHV-urn-muhnt) the people who rule or govern a country or state

mob (MOB) a large and dangerous crowd of people

prairie (PRAIR-ee) a large area of flat or rolling grassland with few or no trees

prisoner (PRIZ-uhn-ur) any person who has been captured or is held

rations (RASH-uhnz) a limited amount or share, especially of food

religion (ri-LIJ-uhn) a specific system of belief, faith, and worship

reservation (rez-ur-VAY-shuhn) an area of land set aside by the government for a special purpose

standoff (STAND-awf) when two equal, opposing sides cannot come to an agreement

survive (sur-VIVE) to continue to live or exist

treaty (TREE-tee) a formal agreement between two or more countries

vision (VIZH-uhn) something that you imagine or dream about

Primary Sources

How can we learn some of the details about Sitting Bull's life? Studying old photographs, drawings, and other things can give us a good look into his world. Since Sitting Bull was an important leader of the Sioux people, his photo was taken. Look at the photo of Sitting Bull and his family on page 29. The photo allows us to identify and describe the kind of clothing and other items that were common to the Sioux Indians in the late nineteenth century.

The drawing on page 31 shows one of the areas where Sitting Bull and his people lived. It was made around the time that Sitting Bull lived there. Notice that there are very few trees in the drawing. By analyzing the picture, we can draw the conclusion that Sitting Bull and his people did not live in wooden houses. Studying sources from the past helps us find the clues to learn about people, places, and events from hundreds of years ago.

Sitting Bull (center) sits with (clockwise) his mother, Her Holy Door; his sister, Good Feather; his daughter, Walks Looking; his other daughter, Has Many Horses; and his grandson, Tan Fly.

The Black Hills of South Dakota are a harsh place. They are very different from the rich, fertile lands where the Lakota had lived for generations.

The buffalo were an important source of food for Sitting Bull's people. They used every part of the animal to make clothes, tools, weapons, and other necessary items.

Sitting Bull's vision of the meadowlark told his future. Meadowlarks are small birds that live in America. Meadowlarks have a special place in Lakota legends. In the legends, they speak the Lakota language and are very respected.